A Rookie reader®

W9-CFD-613

I Need Glasses

Written by Charlie Thomas
Illustrated by Jennifer P. Goldfinger

Children's Press®
A Division of Scholastic Inc.
New York • Toronto • London • Auckland • Sydney
Mexico City • New Delhi • Hong Kong
Danbury, Connecticut

For Paige. No matter how silly or serious,
I am happy to have been able to give you the gift of reading.

For Mike R. Thanks for getting me through this book.
– C.T.

For Nanny, whose glasses I still haven't found.
– J.P.G.

Consultant
Eileen Robinson
Reading Specialist

Library of Congress Cataloging-in-Publication Data

Thomas, Charlie, 1962-
    I need glasses / written by Charlie Thomas ; illustrated by Jennifer P. Goldfinger.
        p. cm. — (A rookie reader)
    Summary: A little girl who cannot find her glasses searches frantically for them so
that she can read a story to her little brother.
    ISBN 0-516-24863-4 (lib. bdg.)   0-516-25024-8 (pbk.)
    [1. Eyeglasses—Fiction. 2. Lost and found possessions—Fiction. 3. Brothers and
sisters—Fiction.] I. Goldfinger, Jennifer P., ill. II. Title. III. Series.
    PZ7.T36633Ian 2005
    [E]—dc22
                                2005003287

Where are my glasses?

I need glasses so I can see. In the daytime, I keep them on the end of my nose.

At night, I put them next to my bed.
I don't want to crush them between
my pillow and my head.

Where are my glasses?

I need glasses to see the starlight.

I need glasses to read my brother bedtime stories.

Where are my glasses?

I need glasses to write
letters to my friends.

Where are my glasses?

I need glasses to draw.

Help! I need my glasses.

Did I leave them near my baseball or basketball?

Did I leave them in
my closet?

Did they fall off in the bathtub?

I need my glasses!

I need my glasses so I can read to you.

Word List (53 words)

(Words in **bold** are compound words.)

and	closet	help	nose	stories
are	crush	I	of	the
at	**daytime**	in	off	them
baseball	did	keep	on	they
basketball	don't	leave	or	to
bathtub	draw	letters	pillow	want
bed	end	my	put	where
bedtime	fall	near	read	write
between	friends	need	see	you
brother	glasses	next	so	
can	head	night	**starlight**	

About the Author

Charlie Thomas has kids, four to be exact. He believes that we have a responsibility to provide our children with the tools to learn and grow, and hopes this book is a part of helping many children embark on the fantastic journey called reading. This is Charlie's first published book, although he's been writing and telling stories to his kids for many years. He resides in Connecticut.

About the Illustrator

Jennifer P. Goldfinger lives in Massachusetts with her husband Michael, and two daughters, Eva and Esme, and their dog Lyle. Jennifer has illustrated several picture books and is the author and illustrator of *A Fish Named Spot.* This is her first *A Rookie Reader®*.